MUSCLE CARS

High Performance: The V8 Revolution

MUSCLE CARS

High Performance: The V8 Revolution

MC

MASON CREST

Nicholas Tomkins

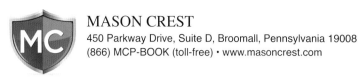

MASON CREST

450 Parkway Drive, Suite D, Broomall, Pennsylvania 19008
(866) MCP-BOOK (toll-free) • www.masoncrest.com

Printed in the United States of America

First printing
9 8 7 6 5 4 3 2 1

ISBN (hardback) 978-1-4222-4416-6
ISBN (series) 978-1-4222-4413-5
ISBN (ebook) 978-1-4222-7396-8

Cataloging-in-Publication Data on file with the Library of Congress

Developed and produced by National Highlights Inc.
Editor: Regency House Publishing Limited
Production: Becki Stewart
Interior and cover design: Regency House Publishing Limited
Text © 2020 Regency House Publishing Limited

QR CODES AND LINKS TO THIRD-PARTY CONTENT

CONTENTS

KEY ICONS TO LOOK OUT FOR:

 Words to Understand: These words with their easy-to-understand definitions will increase the reader's understanding of the text while building vocabulary skills.

 Sidebars: This boxed material within the main text allows readers to build knowledge, gain insights, explore possibilities, and broaden their perspectives by weaving together additional information to provide realistic and holistic perspectives.

 Educational Videos: Readers can view videos by scanning our QR codes, providing them with additional educational content to supplement the text. Examples include news coverage, moments in history, speeches, iconic sports moments, and much more!

 Text-Dependent Questions: These questions send the reader back to the text for more careful attention to the evidence presented there.

 Research Projects: Readers are pointed toward areas of further inquiry connected to each chapter. Suggestions are provided for projects that encourage deeper research and analysis.

 Series Glossary of Key Terms: This back-of-the-book glossary contains terminology used throughout this series. Words found here increase the reader's ability to read and comprehend higher-level books and articles in this field.

INTRODUCTION

What is a muscle car? First of all, let us eliminate what it is not: it is not a piece of Italian exotica, a Ferrari or a Lamborghini, cars which are just too complex and too specialized; nor is it a German Porsche, which is too efficient and too clever by half; nor yet a classic British sports car, a Morgan, TVR, or Jaguar, which could never be regarded as fitting the bill. Sports cars, by and large, are not muscle cars, with two notable exceptions: the legendary AC Cobra of the 1960s, and the Dodge Viper of the 1990s. These followed the muscle car creed of back-to-basics raw power.

In effect, muscle cars always were, and always will be, a quintessentially North American phenomenon. The basic concept is something like this: take a mid-sized American sedan, nothing complex, upscale, or fancy, in fact the sort of car one would use to collect the groceries in any American town on any day of the week; add the biggest, raunchiest V8 that it is possible to squeeze under the hood; and there it is.

Sports cars are not considered to be muscle cars. The exception is the AC Cobra, the English muscle car.

Dodge has been manufacturing muscle cars for years. This is a modern Dodge Viper.

The muscle car concept really is as simple as that. Moreover, the young men who desired these cars, and most of them were young and men, though that would change, were not interested in technical sophistication, nor handling finesse, nor even top speed. Cubic inches, horsepower, and acceleration rates were the only figures that counted. Muscle cars were loud, proud, and in your face, and did not pretend to be anything else. They might have been simple, even crude, but for roaring, pumping, tire-smoking standing starts, they were the business. To an American youth culture raised on drag racing, red-light street racing, and hot-rodding, they were irresistible.

The "Big Three" manufacturers soon woke to this fact and joined the power race to offer more cubic inches, more horsepower, and fewer seconds over the standing quarter. For a few short years, between 1965 and 1970, it seemed as though the race would never end. The result was often more power than the car (and the driver) could handle safely, but then part of the attraction was making a four-seater sedan go faster than it was ever intended.

But the situation could not last. The combination of high horsepower in the hands of young drivers saw accident rates soar, and insurance premiums followed suit. Moreover, the climate of the times was changing, with a whole raft of safety and emissions legislation coming into force in the late 1960s and early 1970s. So, even before the first oil crisis made itself felt, the first-generation muscle cars were already on their way out. By the 1980s, however, they were beginning to creep back, first with turbocharged fours, then V8s; by the 1990s, muscle cars were back with a vengeance: more "high-tech" than before, even sophisticated, with ABS, electronic fuel injection, and multi-valve engines. Manufacturers were by then talking virtuously about catalytic converters and air bags, but the truth was that performance was selling once again. Anti-social? Yes. Irresponsible? Of course. But one thing was certain—the muscle car was back.

The Chevrolet Impala was a prime candidate for a beef-up having been downsized in 1961.

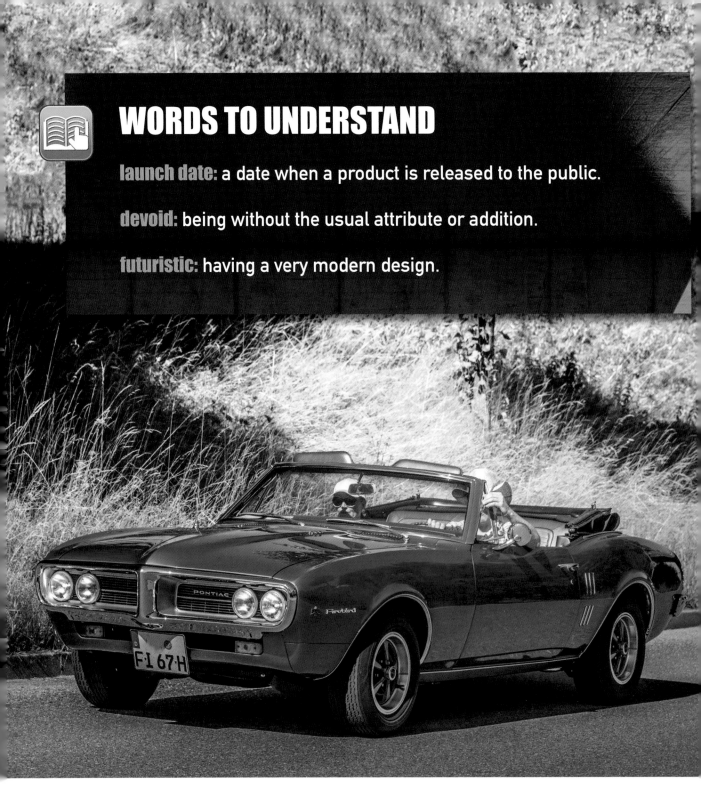

WORDS TO UNDERSTAND

launch date: a date when a product is released to the public.

devoid: being without the usual attribute or addition.

futuristic: having a very modern design.

Pontiac introduced the Firebird in 1967 with the final roll-out in 2002.

CHAPTER 1
PONTIAC FIREBIRD

In many ways, the Pontiac Firebird is the forgotten muscle car. Like every other non-Ford pony car, it was a reaction to the Mustang. General Motors' pony car was really a Chevrolet project, which Pontiac tagged on to late in the day; for the first few years of its life it played second fiddle to its GM sibling, the Chevrolet Camaro. The Firebird, moreover, did not sell as well as its Camaro cousin, let alone the Mustang itself.

And yet the Firebird turned out to be the great survivor among muscle cars, persevering with a big, hairy 455-cu in (7.47-liter) V8 in the uncertain 1970s, when every other muscle car was downsizing, downgrading, or hiding its horsepower beneath a bushel. It was all due to the Trans Am, which started off as a Firebird derivative but ended up

A modified Firebird. Both a two-door hardtop and a convertible were offered in the 1969 model year.

A Firebird 400 in 1968, the second year of production. This is a convertible model.

as a model in its own right. There was a paradox here, too, for the Trans Am, one of America's legendary hot cars, was named after the famous race series but was never a successful racer itself. Yet up to 2002, one could still buy a brand-new Firebird or Trans Am.

In 1964, the Mustang had been let out of its stable and, contrary to the predictions of the industry, was selling in huge numbers. Over at General Motors, Pontiac's top management was peopled by individuals who loved and understood performance cars, most notably Bunkie Knudsen and John DeLorean. In a few short years, they had helped to change Pontiac's image from conservative to hot and desirable, with the Super Duty racing specials. On the back of that, they had recently launched the GTO, which was destined to become the first of a new generation of muscle cars. If any GM division was equipped to meet and beat the Mustang, it was the newly performance-aware Pontiac.

They got to work. Chevrolet had already proposed the XP-836, a sporting four-seater, but John DeLorean in particular wanted a proper two-seat sports car, a cheaper competitor for Chevrolet's own Corvette. This was the XP-833, with a streamlined, **futuristic** plastic body. But it was too avant-garde for GM's top management, who in any case did not want any in-house competition for the Corvette. Consequently, the XP-833 died a swift death.

Meanwhile, Chevrolet had been working hard on the XP-836, the car that would become the Camaro. GM decreed that instead of producing its own Mustang rival, it would work with Chevrolet on the XP-836, which subsequently became a joint project. This put Pontiac at a disadvantage, as Chevrolet was already some months down the design road, and coming to the project so late meant that Pontiac would have little influence on the car's fundamentals. "Pontiac didn't like the decision," wrote Bill Holder and Phillip Kunz in their book *Firebird & Trans Am*, "but that was the way the game would be played." The Camaro's styling had already been finalized, and to cut costs (and time) the new Pontiac would have to share its wings and doors: only the nose and tail could be altered to make the car different in character from the Camaro.

They managed to do this by giving it a GTO-style split-front grille with recessed twin headlights and narrow rear lights in two tiers, instead of the Camaro's conventional lights. It was not much, but at least the cars now looked like cousins rather than clones. The downside was that the extra design work pushed the Pontiac's **launch date** back to February 1967, five months after that of the Camaro. However, the Firebird did have a suitably evocative name.

The engine of a 1968 Firebird 400.

Late Starter

"After this," went the advertising copy, "you'll never go back to driving whatever you're driving." That ran below an almost full-page color picture of an open-top Firebird 400 roaring along an open mountain road, **devoid** of traffic (in car advertisements, roads never have any other traffic). The advertisement also referred to "400 cubes of chromed V8…heavy-duty 3-speed floor shift, extra-sticky suspension, and a set of duals that announce your coming like the brass section of the New York Philharmonic." If Pontiac was attempting to sell a politically incorrect fantasy, it was doing a pretty good job.

That 400 was the top model of five: Firebird, Sprint, 326, 326HO, and 400. The base model came in at only $2,600, powered by Pontiac's own overhead-cam 230-cu in (3.77-liter) straight six with 165 hp (123 kW). Despite all the components it shared with the Camaro, the Firebird used Pontiac's own power units. That also allowed Pontiac to offer the Sprint, which was surely unique among muscle cars in using a highly tuned six-cylinder engine instead of a

A 1969 Firebird.

High Performance: The V8 Revolution

A 1970 Firebird 400.

V8. For only $116 extra over the base Firebird, the straight six was given a Rochester four-barrel carburetor, higher-lift cam, 10.5:1 compression ratio, split exhaust manifold, and freer-flowing air cleaner, plus 215 hp (160 kW), 50 hp (37 kW) more than standard. As part of the package, the three-speed shifter was floor-mounted, and the suspension was firmed up. By American standards, this was a relatively small-engined high-revving performance car. Both the Sprint and base Firebird could be had in open-top forms, as a $237 option. Despite that seductive advertisement, convertibles were only ever a minority of Firebird sales: fewer than 16,000 were sold in that first year, or about one-fifth of the total.

If the Sprint seemed too frenetic, and for many traditionalists it probably did, the more laid-back 326-cu in (5.34-liter) V8 was a better choice. Slightly more powerful than the Sprint at 250 hp (186.5 kW), but with far more torque as it provided 330 lb ft (447.5 Nm) at 2,800 rpm, this was the most relaxed of the new Firebirds. Pontiac underlined the point by equipping it with a non-sporting three-speed column shifter, and billing the buyer for $21 less than the Sprint owner. A three-speed transmission was not synonymous with boulevard cruising: even the top-performance Firebird 400 stuck with a three-speed. For an extra $47, Firebird 326 owners could make that a floor shift, while a center console and bucket seats were also on the options list. As ever, the interior design of mass-market muscle cars

BUNKIE KNUDSEN

Semon Emil "Bunkie" Knudsen was born in Buffalo, New York, in 1912. His father, William S. Knudsen, was a three-star general and also a former president of General Motors. William's enthusiam for automobiles passed on to his son Bunkie, who became interested in all things mechanical. Even as a teenager, Bunkie was an accomplished mechanic, able to fix or even assemble an automobile. Bunkie joined General Motors in 1939 and then quickly rose through the ranks to top management in the company. In 1968, Bunkie moved to Ford, but political infighting led to his dismissal in 1969. Bunkie Knudsen died in 1998 in Bloomfield Hills, Michigan.

Scan here to take a closer look at the Firebird 400 Ram Air.

was just as important as the way they looked on the outside. Owners were paying for something that made them feel special. Not for nothing had the Camaro's designers aimed for a fighter plane feel for the interior.

But it was the two top Firebirds, the 400 and the 326HO, that finally entered true muscle car territory. The HO took the standard 326-cu in engine and added a 10.5:1 compression, Carter four-barrel carburetor, and dual exhaust, among other things. According to Pontiac, this boosted power by a modest 14 percent to 285 hp (212.5 kW). This figure is generally considered to have been under-rated, with the true figure at 300 hp (224 kW) or more. The official torque figure seems more believable, at 359 lb ft (486.8 Nm). To proclaim to the world that one had bought an HO, the car sported long body stripes and "HO" badges: in this instance, the HO stood for "High Output".

At the end of that first 1967 model year, 82,560 Firebirds had found buyers, which was surely not as many as Pontiac would have liked, but the car was hamstrung by missing the first five months of the sales season. That was partly why Chevrolet managed to sell over 200,000 Camaros in the same year. Both were a long way off Mustang figures, but the figures were good enough. And in 1968, the Firebird's first full year on sale, 107,000 cars were sold. In fact, 1968 would head the Firebird's sales record for eight years. This, of course, was the height of the muscle car boom; only a few short years into the future, and Pontiac salesmen would be looking back to these times with feelings of nostalgia.

There were few major changes in that year. The straight six got a capacity boost to 250 cu in (4.1 liters) which gave 175 hp (130.5 kW) and 240 lb ft (325.4 Nm), though it was still a mildly tuned unit, with a lowly 9.0:1 compression ratio. Oddly, although the Sprint enjoyed the same increase in cubes, it was still quoted at 215 hp (160 kW), though rated torque was up to 255 lb ft (345.8 Nm): maybe the original had proved just a little too "European" for traditional U.S. buyers. Of more significance was the replacement of the 326-cu in unit with the Firebird 350. Like its predecessor, this 350-cu in (5.74-liter) V8 came in two forms: mild-mannered cruiser with a single two-barrel carburetor, three-speed column shifter and now 265 hp (197.5 kW) at 4,600 rpm, and as the 350HO with four-barrel Rochester, 10.5:1 compression, and 320 hp (238.5 kW). As with the original HO, there were plenty of cues on the outside as to what lay beneath the hood, such as dual exhaust and F70 x 14 tires, plus all the usual stripes and badges. The 350HO's power output was not far behind that of the 400, now boosted slightly to 335 hp (250 kW) at

A striking 1971 Firebird.

A 1973 Pontiac Firebird convertible.

5,000rpm as the 400HO and still offered with or without Ram Air. This was due to a higher 10.75:1 compression and power-flex fan. Any performance difference between the 350 and 400 engines may have been small, but for many buyers there was still one very good reason to pay the extra $435 for a 400: it still had more cubes than any other pony car—even the latest 1968 Camaro had only 396. Of course, that could be coaxed up to 375 hp (279.5 kW) with a dealer-fitted hot camshaft. The Z28 Camaro produced 400 hp (298 kW), but for many buyers, the Firebird 400 remained the cubic-capacity king. To maintain interest, Pontiac offered an updated Ram Air system, the Ram Air II, late in the model year, though the real significance lay not in the Ram Air itself, but in the fact that the new engine was significantly stronger than the old one, with forged pistons and four-bolt main bearings.

Any doubts Pontiac may have had about adopting and adapting what was basically a Chevrolet design would have been banished by a six-car test in *Car and Driver* during May 1968. A Firebird 400HO was compared with a Camaro SS396, AMC Javelin SST, Mustang 2+2 GT, Mercury Cougar XR-7, and Plymouth Barracuda Formula S. The Pontiac product came out head and shoulders above them all.

Car and Driver loved its big engine, though admittedly it had been very well prepared, and scored it top of the six in every category. It was the fastest-accelerating of the six, and by some margin, attaining 60 mph (96.5 km/h) in 5.5

seconds when compared with the 6.6 and 6.3 seconds recorded by the Camaro and Mustang, respectively, and the quarter-mile time of 14.2 seconds. Moreover, it revved so quickly and smoothly that it was easy to overshoot the 5,100 rpm shift point. The variable-ratio power steering (the first on an American-made pony car) came in for particular praise, as did the handling. There was no mention of the axle hop, which early Firebird tests criticized, so the changes for 1968 (multi-leaf springs and staggered shocks) seem to have worked. The ride was thought to be a little too firm, but the Firebird scored bottom only on front fender protection and the effectiveness of its wipers, hardly major points. When all the points were added up, the Firebird scored 118, ahead of the Barracuda (111), Javelin (91), Cougar (90), Camaro (79), and Mustang (73).

"For sheer enjoyment and confidence behind the wheel," the *Car and Driver* testers concluded, "the Firebird was almost in a class of itself." By contrast, the Camaro was "built to be all things to all people, and as a result, it was a disappointment." That surely was the sweetest victory for the Pontiac engineers. They had succeeded in taking a Chevrolet design and transforming it through careful use of their own components. As *Car and Driver* acknowledged, the division seemed to have a knack for taking unpromising material and producing something very different. If *Car and Driver*'s test was to be believed, it certainly succeeded with the Firebird.

A 1973 Firebird Sprint with a vinyl top.

TEXT- DEPENDENT QUESTIONS

1. What book did Bill Holder and Phillip Kunz write?

2. Explain why 1964 was a good year for Ford Mustang sales.

3. How many Firebirds were sold by the end of 1967?

By 1973, the Firebird's fenders were color coded.

A 1970s Firebird performing a wheelie on a drag racing track.

RESEARCH PROJECT

Write a one-page essay explaining why the Firebird became such an iconic muscle car of the 1960s.

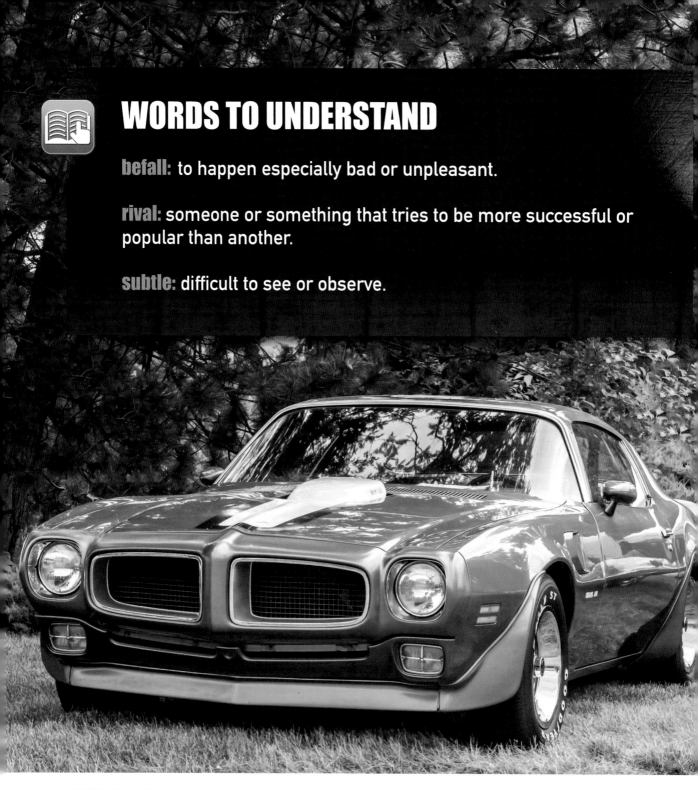

WORDS TO UNDERSTAND

befall: to happen especially bad or unpleasant.

rival: someone or something that tries to be more successful or popular than another.

subtle: difficult to see or observe.

A 1970 Trans Am.

CHAPTER PONTIAC TRANS AM 2

It had not escaped the Pontiac management that the Mustang had come last in that *Car and Driver* test. The reason was simple: the Mustang had barely changed in three years, while newer **rivals** were coming thick and fast. They were determined that no such fate should **befall** the Firebird, so for 1969, after less than two years on the market, the Firebird received some major changes. As well as the **subtle** alterations to the sheet metal enjoyed by the Camaro that year, the Firebird's front end was restyled, with the quad headlights now carried in body-colored moldings, with the famous split grille squeezed inward to make room. Inside, there were an improved dashboard and new safety features.

The Sprint got a power boost to 230 hp (171.5 kW), but the best-seller of the entire range remained the softer Firebird 350, its power unchanged. The 350HO could boast an extra 5 hp (3.75 kW), which was not much, but it counted on the all-important specification sheet, to 325 hp (242 kW), as a result of new cylinder heads, larger valves, and a higher lift cam. The base 400 now offered only 5 hp more than the 350, but 13 percent more torque at 430 lb ft

A Pontiac Trans Am Ram Air engine.

(583.1 Nm). It were also given all the visual cues of the largest-engined Firebird on offer: hood scoops (which was available even without Ram Air), dual exhausts, and a floor shifter. An extra $435 brought Ram Air III, which gave those hood scoops something to do, and according to Pontiac delivered an extra 5 hp and identical torque to the standard 400. If that was not enough, there was a new Ram Air IV for 1969. It was expensive at $832 extra (and not many were sold) but promised much, with a hotter cam, aluminum cylinder heads, and different valve train. Another clue as to why not many Firebird customers chose to check the Ram Air IV box lay in Pontiac's official power figures, which put Ram Air IV at 345 hp (257 kW) at 5,400 rpm, with identical torque. Most considered that 10 hp (7.45 kW) more for $800 was not an outstanding deal. However, the very same engine in Pontiac's GTO was quoted at 370 hp

A late 1970s Trans Am.

(276 kW). Either Pontiac had made a slip, which was unlikely, was being modest, which was very unlikely, or wanted to take the heat off its top-performance car in the face of the criticisms of safety campaigners.

Whatever the truth, it was overshadowed by a new option for the Firebird that, with hindsight, was more significant than any of those: the Trans Am. Mention that name today, and most people will not think of the race series for pony cars, but a hot Pontiac that made the name its own. Pontiac's plan went like this: it did not have a suitable competitive engine for the popular Trans Am series, so it started to develop a 303-cu in (4.965-liter) V8 based on the 400. In the meantime, Firebirds were raced using Z28 Camaro power units. After racing a while, the special 303 would be fitted to a road-going Trans Am named after the series. But it took too long to develop, and

JOHN DELOREAN AND THE PONTIAC FIREBIRD

John Zachary DeLorean was an American engineer famous for his contribution toward the development of a number of iconic vehicles, including the Pontiac Firebird. The Firebird was a an affordable compact pony car with fantastic looks. It was produced as a rival to the Ford Mustang. The Firebird had powerful and performance-orientated engineering, so consquently, the model was a hit with the youthful automobile market. Over the years, the Firebird came with many special options, including bigger engines, special editions, and better trim. The Firebird was the base model in the series, but there were also GTO, Trans Am, and Ram Air versions.

Scan here to watch a video about a 1978 Pontiac Trans Am Bandit 6.6 Classic.

by the time 303 was ready, the rules had changed, and it was not legal for Trans Am racing.

Faced with race-heritage rivals like the Z28 and Boss Mustangs, moreover, Pontiac did not want to delay its road-going spin-off, so the Firebird Trans Am was launched anyway, at the Chicago Auto Show in March 1969, though powered by the existing 400-cu in motor rather than the special 303. Consequently, when it was launched, the new Trans Am had never actually turned a wheel on a race track. Pontiac even had to pay the Sports Car Club of America a $5 royalty on every car. Still, it was a good investment, given that the car was still going strong 30 years later and was better known than the race series!

So, what was the basis of the Trans Am? It seems almost sacrilegious to suggest it, but without that special 303-cu in race-bred engine, the early Trans Am was little more than a Firebird 400 with a spoiler and a different paint job. Engine-wise it was identical to the top 400s, with 335-hp (250-kW) Ram Air III or so-called 345-hp (257-kW) Ram Air IV. It looked very different, however, and this was part of its reason for being. John DeLorean was the power behind the Trans Am. As GM's Pontiac chief, he could not help but notice how well the Z28 Camaro had been selling. What the Firebird needed was its very own Z28, and the project that was initiated was code named "Pontiac Firebird Sprint Turismo."

When launched, the Trans Am looked as though it would be loud even before it was started up. All the early cars came in white, with blue racing stripes running the length of the hood, roof, and trunk lid. Two grand scoops gaped hungrily out of the hood, two more extractor scoops were fitted just behind each front wheel, and there was a large rear spoiler, which the engineers calculated to produce 100 lb (45 kg) of down-force at 100 mph (161 km/h). So the Trans Am was flashy (tame by the standards of the 1970s, but a rabid extrovert for its time), but there were some suspension changes over the standard Firebird as well, namely heavy-duty springs, a 1-in (2.54-cm) stabilizer bar and 7-in (17.8-cm) wheels. It was not a mere paint-and-badges job, but it was close.

Nor was the first Trans Am a mass-market car. Pontiac made only 697 in its first year, most of which were fitted with Ram Air III, and most were automatics. But despite the extra glamour of the Trans Am, Ram Air IV, and the restyling, Firebird sales as a whole were actually down in 1969, to 87,000, and that was over an extended 15-month model year, as a strike delayed the launch of the 1970 cars.

A 1978 Firebird Trans Am.

A 1979 Trans Am.

For 1970, the Firebird, and of course the Trans Am, shared new single-headlight styling with the Camaro: the Chevrolet and Pontiac vehicles would share bodies until 1981. Most people liked the cleaner look, with more subtle hood scoops and an inbuilt rear spoiler on the top Formula 400. But the times were reflected in other changes. To rationalize and save money, Pontiac's overhead-cam six was dropped in favor of the equivalent Chevrolet six, which brought the power down to 155 hp (115.5 kW). The peppy Sprint was replaced by the Esprit, which made luxury, rather than performance, its top selling point. It was powered by the 350 V8, now with lower 8.8:1 compression and single two-barrel carburetor, producing 255 hp (190 kW). Meanwhile, the three 400-powered Firebirds were replaced by the Formula 400, offered with either the 330-hp (246-kW) base-model engine or the 335-hp (250-kW) Ram Air III. Ram Air IV was now only available to special order. The Formula's suspension was upgraded along Trans Am lines, with front and rear stabilizer bars and heavy-duty springs.

The 1970 Trans Am ("1970+" in official Pontiac jargon as it had been launched late, in March 1970) went along with the more subtle approach of the Firebirds. The rear spoiler was the muted, inbuilt unit seen on the Formula, and new front spoiler (giving up to 50 lb/23 kg of downforce according to Pontiac) was also smoothly styled in. The standard power unit was Ram Air III; here again, Ram IV was available on special order, but was taken up by only 88 Trans Am buyers. Nevertheless, they still got a Shaker hood (in place of the twin front-facing scoops), Rally II wheels, power brakes and steering, concealed wipers, and dual horns, while the front stabilizer bar was a beefier 1.25 in (3.175 cm). The changes worked, and more than 3,000 Trans Ams were sold in that year. This was not enough to worry Ford or anyone else, but it was a useful boost to the Firebird, whose sales collapsed disastrously in 1970 to fewer than 46,000, or half the 1969 figure. The muscle car bubble had burst, but could the Pontiacs cope?

The Pontiac Trans Am featured in the movie Smokey and The Bandit *that showcased the car. The cars used in the movie were equipped with 400-cu in V8 engines and had removable t-bar roof panels.*

A late 1970s Trans Am.

TEXT- DEPENDENT QUESTIONS

1. What changes were made to the Firebird in 1969?

2. What car was launched at the Chicago Auto Show in 1969?

3. What model replaced the Sprint?

RESEARCH PROJECT

Using the Internet, find out how you would go about finding a classic car to buy. List the pros and cons of owning a 1960s or a 1970s automobile.

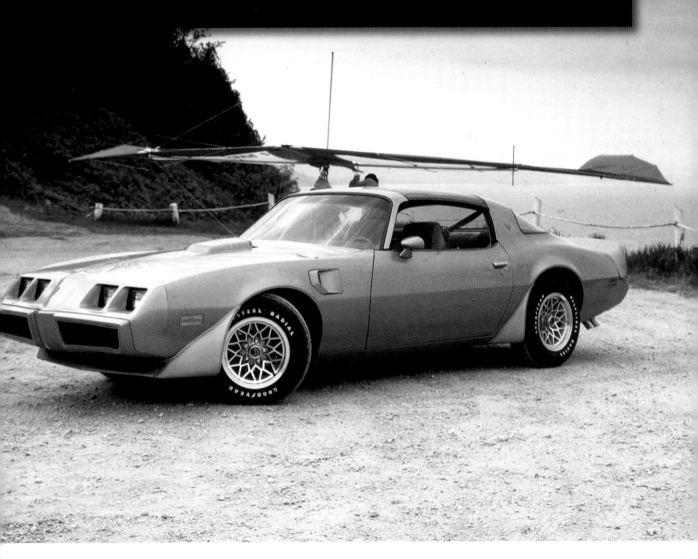

A 1979 Trans Am with its four rectangular headlights.

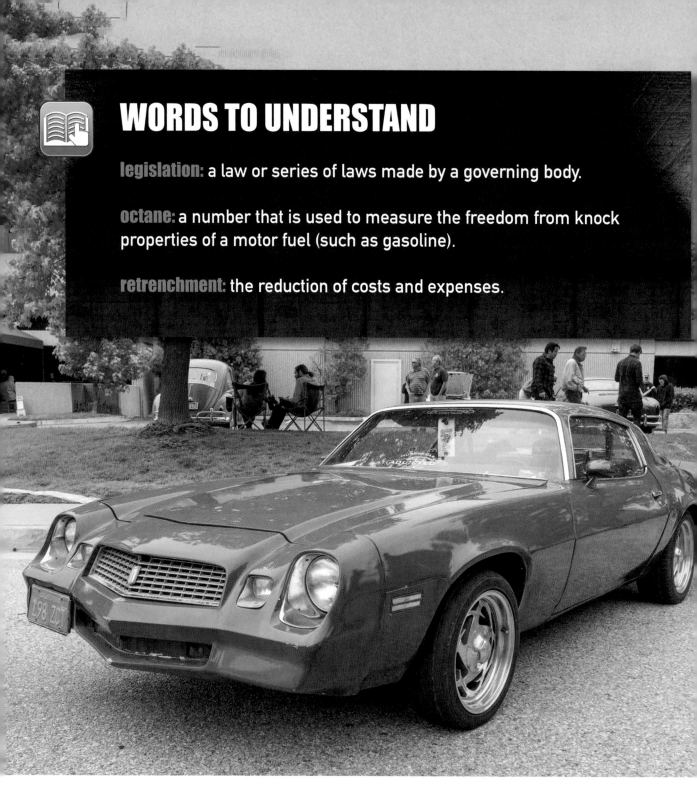

WORDS TO UNDERSTAND

legislation: a law or series of laws made by a governing body.

octane: a number that is used to measure the freedom from knock properties of a motor fuel (such as gasoline).

retrenchment: the reduction of costs and expenses.

Pontiac produced the Trans Am with a 455 cu in engine from 1971 to 1976.

CHAPTER 3

THE 455

In many ways, Pontiac made the same efforts at **retrenchment** as every other muscle car manufacturer in the early 1970s. Compression ratios were scaled back to cope with lower-**octane** fuel and stricter emission limits, and there was as much emphasis on luxury muscle (in the new Esprit Firebird, for example) as on sheer horsepower. The whole atmosphere had changed as horsepower figures tumbled. Much of the latter was the result of a change in measurement from gross to net horsepower, but it served only to reinforce the idea that the performance car was retreating.

In the midst of all this, Pontiac launched the biggest-ever V8 fitted to a pony car, a 455-cu in (7.46-liter) unit. Fitted only to the Formula Firebird or the Trans Am, it came in two guises: 8.2:1 compression for 325 hp (242 kW) gross or 255 hp (190 kW) net, or 8.4:1 and a four-barrel carburetor HO with 335 hp (265 kW). Naturally, these massive motors pushed out a great deal of torque, and even the low-compression version managed 455 lb ft (617 Nm): in other words, one pound per foot per cubic inch, more likely to have been the result of careful development rather than sheer coincidence.

If the 455s seemed over the top, one could still buy a Formula 400 (now detuned to 300 hp/224 kW gross or 250 hp/186.5 kW net) with a lower-powered, budget-priced Formula 350, which cost only $29 more than the Esprit. The idea of the new, cheaper Formula was to provide all the performance add-ons (bucket seats, suspension package, hood scoops) with lower purchase, insurance, and running costs. With this car and the 455s, Pontiac was offering Firebirds in tune with the incoming tide of safety and emissions **legislation**, but at the same time struggling to come to terms with the inevitable.

The Esprit, meanwhile, came with 350 or 400 two-barrel V8s, both in modest states of tune, and buyers of the basic Firebird had a choice of the 250-cu in (4.18-liter) straight six or the 350. Not surprisingly, the Trans Am came only with the new 455 motor, but delivered 33 5hp at 3,500 rpm and 480 lb ft (650.9 Nm). In fact, despite the hard times for muscle cars, there were more Firebird models to choose from than ever before. Not that it helped sales much. They were up marginally, to 53,000 (excluding just over 2,100 Trans Ams) but, to put that in perspective, the Pontiac was outsold by the Camaro and Mustang by three to one.

The year 1972 proved to be the Firebird/Trans Am's low point: this was in fact the year that GM considered dropping both the Chevrolet and Pontiac pony cars, though both just managed to survive. In keeping with the times, the best-selling model was the basic Firebird, which made up 40 percent of the 1972 total. It still came with a choice of detuned 250-cu in six (now derated to 110 hp/82 kW net) or two-barrel 350-cu in (5.74-liter) V8 offering 160 hp (119 kW). It was closely followed by the Esprit (still majoring on chrome and interior fittings), now available with a 400 V8 as well as the 350. And the performance Formula? This had greater engine choice than ever before: 160- or 175-hp (119- or 130.5-kW), 250-hp (186.5-kW) 400 or 300-hp (224-kW) 455. Despite these options, only a little over 5,000 vehicles were sold, so despite the extra choice and the reflected glamour of the Trans Am, it seemed as though buyers really were abandoning muscle cars. The Trans Am itself came only with that top 455 motor, and about two-thirds of buyers opted for the M-40 automatic rather than the Hurst shifter four-speed manual.

The power figures seemed low, but all were net horsepower, so for performance freaks things were not as bad as they appeared: a Formula 455, for instance, could still run the quarter-mile in 14 seconds, so it was no slower than its predecessors. All well and good, but fewer than 1,300 Trans Ams trickled off the production line (a result, in part, of

An early 1970s 455.

Pontiac also produced the 400 in the 1970s.

labor problems) and sales of the whole range amounted to 28,700. It was little wonder that the GM top brass considered dropping the whole lot.

But having decided to hang on in, Pontiac took no half-measures. For 1973, while almost every other muscle car was in retreat, the Firebird and Trans Am were given extra power. It came in the form of the SD-455 V8, which was the existing 455 with many tweaks and changes to produce 310 hp (231 kW) net. That was equivalent to around 350 hp (261 kW) gross, so this 1973 V8 was offering the same sort of power as muscle cars of the late 1960s. To underline a return to what some would see as the good old days, Pontiac resurrected the "SD" or "Super Duty" tag, the name given to all those drag racing special parts of the early 1960s.

SD was no misnomer, as it was a very different motor from the standard 455, with a reinforced block, forged rods, aluminum pistons, Quadra Jet carburetor, dry sump lubrication, special cam, four-bolt main bearings, and dual exhaust. In fact, so hot was the SD that it failed to meet emission limits, and Pontiac had to hurriedly derate it by 20 hp (14.9 kW). With a milder cam and cleaner exhaust, it could manage 290 hp (216 kW), still more than any other muscle car. Moreover, the Firebird/Trans Am still had more cubic inches than any rival, and for some people these things still counted. In the Trans Am, the SD-455 came with beefed-up three-speed Hydra-Matic (with the shift point raised to 5,400 rpm), a heavy duty-radiator, and uprated suspension. Oddly enough, having produced a hot car in a cold era, Pontiac seemed a little shy of the fact. One Trans Am 455 buyer recalled that he "had to beg" for his car, and wait five months for delivery. And he also had to pay $675 extra for the privilege, which was quite a chunk of money

A customized late 1970 Trans Am at a car show in Germany.

in 1973. Pontiac's reticence was at odds with the hottest Trans Am yet, especially with its new-for-1973 big bird decal, which now covered the entire hood.

Originally, the SD-455 was to have been a Trans Am option only, but Pontiac decided to offer it on the Firebird Formula as well, which continued with the standard 455, 400, and 350 V8s. As ever, the Formula offered a good-value performance package: for only $27 more than the Esprit, buyers got a twin-scoop hood, heavy-duty suspension, dual exhausts, and several other bits and pieces. But as if to atone for the SD, other Firebird power plants were derated in that year, with lower compressions: the base 250-cu in six was down to 100 hp (74.5 kW), and only 10 percent of base Firebird customers chose it. Most went for the torquier 350 V8. In fact, the best-seller in 1973 was not that one, nor the sporty Formula, still less the flamboyant Trans Am, but the luxury Esprit. All told, Pontiac produced just over 46,000 Firebirds and Trans Ams for 1973, so the SD had not reversed the decline.

In fact, 1974 would be the SD's second and final year. Although applauded by the performance freaks, it really was swimming against the tide: gas was getting expensive, and it almost seemed unpatriotic to waste the stuff. Fewer than 1,000 Trans Am SDs were sold in 1974, and a mere 58 Formula SDs (evidently, there were not enough performance freaks around). But sales of less-macho Firebird/Trans Ams actually rose that year, to well over 70,000. Once again, the luxury Esprit was the best-seller, followed by the base Firebird, the Formula and, bringing up the rear,

RISING GAS PRICES IN THE 1970S

The 1970s saw a steep rise in gas prices coupled with tightening safety regulations. So, like other muscle car classics of the time such as the Mustang and the Corvette, the Firebird's raw early engine units were soon tamed, making their performance more constrained and muted. Even their styling became more modern and efficient. Only later and following extensive research, more advanced engine technologies were able to replace some of the power lost from the early V8s. It is interesting to note that today's performance cars are considerably more efficient, faster, safer, and economical than the cars of the 1960s, 1970s, and 1980s.

Scan here to watch a video about the Trans Am SD-455.

the Trans Am. The Trans Am package had become comprehensive and was no rebadged Firebird: power steering, front discs, limited-slip differential, Rally gauges, Rally II wheels, sport suspension, and many other parts were all standard. Even with the milder-sloping front end fitted to all Firebird/Trans Ams in that year, it looked the part.

There are two ways of looking at the Firebird/Trans Am in the mid-1970s. Enthusiasts would bemoan the dropping of first the SD-455, then the basic 455 (though it would return in derated form), with ever lower compression ratios and power outputs for the other engines. On the other hand, Pontiac were selling more Firebird/Trans Ams than ever before. In 1974, the Trans Am became the best-seller, with over 27,000 sold, while the following year combined sales exceeded 110,000, a significant milestone. There were few important changes to the actual cars, more a juggling of engine options to give more choice to base and Esprit buyers, and more emphasis on the Formula's appearance than its quarter-mile times. The base Firebird, for example, actually got a slight power boost in 1976, to 110 hp (82 kW), the choice of 160- or 175-hp (119- or 130.5-kW) 350 V8s and, for the first time, the 185-hp (138-kW) 400. Meanwhile, the Trans Am was still the best-selling model, with over 46,000 finding homes. Even more significant for Pontiac's sibling rivalry with Chevrolet, the Trans Am was now outselling the Corvette. In short, it had become a muscle car model in its own right, and from that point on, "Trans Am" would be just as recognizable as "Firebird."

TEXT- DEPENDENT QUESTIONS

1. Name the two 455-cu in (7.46-liter) units lauched by Pontiac.

2. Name the two types of Esprit engines.

3. What does SD stand for?

A 1977 Trans Am.

The black-and-gold paint job was a classic for Trans Ams of the late 1970s.

RESEARCH PROJECT

Make a list of five famous muscle cars used in movies or TV shows.

WORDS TO UNDERSTAND

decade: a period of ten years.

fluctuate: to rise and fall irregularly in number or amount.

sales boom: a rapid and significant growth in sales.

A late Trans Am of the 1980s.

CHAPTER 4
BOOM & BUST

In the late 1970s, both the Trans Am and Firebird enjoyed a **sales boom**, with over 150,000 cars (almost 70,000 of them Trans Ams) sold in 1977 alone. Well over 200,000 found homes in 1979. It is hard to say why this happened. With the 455 V8 finally gone, the Pontiac pony was following all the other muscle cars down the road of lower compressions and fewer cubic inches, though looks must have had a lot to do with the car's success. Pontiac's pony still looked the part of a true muscle car, especially in Trans Am form or as the Formula with its optional W50 body

A 1980 Trans Am GTA.

package. Trans Am special editions in black and gold, or Firebird Esprits in bright blue or red, all with loud decals and stripes, were also popular.

Recognized by its four rectangular headlights, Trans Am/Firebirds of this era also saw some significant engine changes. The faithful straight six was replaced by a 231-cu in (3.785-liter) V6, sourced from Buick, in two- or four-barrel forms. Meanwhile, a small-block V8 of 305 cu in (5.0 liters) was brought in from Chevrolet, offering 145 hp (108 kW). The familiar 400 continued but was topped by a 403-cu in (6.6-liter) V8 with 220 hp (164 kW): it was not a 455, but certainly on the way there.

To celebrate its tenth birthday in 1979, the Trans Am enjoyed its best sales figure yet, at 117,000. On the tenth anniversary special edition, there was a bigger bird on the hood, silver leather bucket seats, and a silver-tinted hatch roof. The pure convertible had long since gone, replaced by an optional T-roof. The special edition also celebrated the fact that, once again, the Trans Am had been chosen as the official pace car for the Daytona 500; this always impressed the buying public, and Pontiac made the most of the fact with pace car replicas.

In the following year, however, both Trans Am and Firebird sales slumped. Was it because the big 400 and 403 V8s had been dropped? Possibly it was, though the 301-cu in (4.93-liter) turbo V8 that replaced them was almost as

A late 1980s Trans Am at a drag race.

THE FOURTH-GENERATION

The fourth-generation Firebirds were manufactured from 1993 to 2002. They were known for their aerodynamic styling inherited from the previous generation. There were many aspects of this model that were the same as before, including the rear axle, floorpan, and front seats. However, most of the new Firebird's styling was upated. Major improvements included standard dual airbags, four-wheel anti-lock brakes, updated wheels, rack-and-pinion power steering, improved suspension, and non-rusting body panels. Five-speed manual transmission was standard with the V6s, and a six-speed manual for the V8s. A four-speed automatic was optional, featuring built-in electronic controls beginning in 1994.

 Scan here to watch a video about a 1980 Trans Am.

powerful, at 210 hp (156.5 kW). That 301 had become the standard power plant, available in 140- and 155-hp (104- and 115.5-kW) forms alongside a single V6, and of course, the 210-hp turbo. Once again, there was a Daytona pace car replica, and over 5,000 of these were sold. But maybe the Trans Am/Firebird was simply looking old: after all, the basic design stretched back over a decade, and in 1981 sales had slumped again. Pontiac needed a new one.

It arrived in the following year, with a sleeker, cleaner all-new body shape that nevertheless managed to retain a family resemblance to the old Firebird. With more attention given to aerodynamics, there were a steeply raked windshield and squared-off tail, while the new car weighed 2,800 lb (1270 kg), significantly lighter than the old one. Pontiac was following Ford's example with the new Mustang: shaving off weight to keep up performance with less power and better economy than the old-style muscle cars. Like the Mustang, the base power unit was a four-cylinder 153-cu in (2.5-liter) motor, the "Iron Duke", with a mid-range 171-cu in (2.8-liter) V6 and, for the Trans Am, a 150-hp (112-kW) 305-cu in (5.0-liter) V8. For 1983, a V6 HO was added, with 135 hp (100.5 kW), while the V8 came with a choice of carburetor or fuel injection. There was a special edition, too, the 25th Anniversary Daytona 500 Pace Car, plus the black-and-gold Recaro Trans Am with special interior and an extra $3,610 on the dealer's bill.

By and large, buyers liked the new cars, though sales did **fluctuate** through the 1980s. They soared the first year, dipped in 1983 then soared again to nearly 130,000. In 1985 they were down again, falling to less than 100,000.

There were just three models: base Firebird, S/E, and Trans Am, the last of which remained the best-seller, making up nearly half of all sales. The two top models were face lift for 1985, with new front and rear ends, with the new look especially dramatic on the Trans Am with its optional W62 ground effects package. This was clearly inspired by racing, with aerodynamic "skirts" as well as the usual front and rear spoilers. They might have reduced ground clearance, but who cared? Perhaps more significant was the rebirth of performance.

Along with other muscle cars of the mid- and late-1980s, the Trans Am began once again to offer big horsepower figures. The 305-cu in (5.0-liter) V8 now came in three versions: base, HO, and TPI (Tuned Port Injection) with 155 hp (115.5 kW), 190 hp (141.5 kW) and 205 hp (153 kW) respectively. Performance, it seemed, was back in fashion. Even cubic inches were making a comeback, and for 1987 Pontiac fitted a 350-cu in (5.735-liter) V8 with 210 hp (156.5 kW). The engine was from Chevrolet, but Pontiac needed it to counter the new 5.0-liter V8 Mustang. It was hardly surprising to learn that the 2.5-liter four-cylinder Firebird had been dropped.

There was a multiplicity of options to go with the new-found performance. The Y99 suspension package, for example (front and rear stabilizer bars with custom shocks), and a whole range of rear axle ratios. For 1988, the

A late 1980s Trans Am at a drag race.

This is a replica of the "Kitt" Trans Am which was used in the 1980s show Nightrider.

350-cu in TPI V8 was up to 235 hp (175 kW), available both in Trans Am and a reborn Formula, while there was a new GTA, which slotted in midway between those two. This was a sort of performance Firebird, with a whole range of options like all-wheel disc brakes and performance suspension to turn it into a budget Trans Am. It was a popular car, with over 20,000 built. Once again, the Trans Am enjoyed pace car status in 1989, though the replica, of which more than 5,700 were sold, used a turbo V6 rather than one of the big-cube V8s. In actual fact, it was more powerful than any of them, with 245 hp (183 kW).

On the face of it, the Trans Am and Firebird seemed to have moved with the times. Lighter and more efficient than the old-school muscle cars, but now with big performance once again, from a choice of V8s offering 200 hp (149 kW) or more. They looked the part too, muscular, but aerodynamic, and clean. And yet the honeymoon was over. From 1987, sales fell year on year, falling to even greater depths than the dark days of the early 1970s. Pontiac sold over 110,000 pony cars in 1986, little more than half that in 1989 and a little over 20,000 in 1990. Nor was the Trans Am the tower of strength it once had been: it became a minority seller in the range, with less than 2,500 sold in 1990. Sales did recover slightly in 1991, thanks to a complete restyle front and rear, and a new convertible option across the range, while the 5.7-liter TPI V8 came in 205-, 230-, and 240-hp (153-, 171.5-, and 179-kW) forms. For economy-minded buyers, there was still a 3.1-liter injected V6. But it was a temporary blip, and sales slumped again in 1992, despite a 25th Anniversary Trans Am and the special Firehawk. The latter was a hot, high-priced rival to the ZR1 Corvette, with 350 hp (261 kW) and 390 lb ft (528.8 Nm) from its tuned 5.7-liter V8. Add in competition options like Recaro seats and a Simpson five-point harness, and the Firehawk could cost as much as $50,000.

The Final Generation

The fifth-generation Firebird/Trans Am appeared in 1993. Now with rounded 1990s styling, to the casual observer it was little different from any other sports 2+2 of the time. And as ever, Pontiac's pony was little more than a restyled Chevrolet Camaro. It shared the new body and its 350 V8 with that eternal arch-rival, the only styling differences being below the waistline. Still, there was no denying that it was substantially new, with only 10 per cent of its parts carried over from the old car. The 1990s Firebird was still a rear-wheel-drive V8-powered 2+2, and in that at least little had changed.

Under the skin, a whole range of safety equipment included ABS brakes, plus driver and safety airbags. There were just two basic engines, a 160-hp (119-kW) 207-cu in (3.4-liter) V6 and a 280-hp (209-kW) 5.7-liter V8. But the high-performance Firehawk had proved so popular that this returned, now with a fuel-injected LT1 power unit of 300 hp (224 kW) and the choice of six-speed manual or four-speed automatic transmission. Customers could expect a 13.5-second quarter-mile, so if there had been any doubt that performance was back in fashion, here was the proof.

As ever, there were both Firebirds and Trans Ams; for 1994 the former came with the V6 or a 275-hp (205-kW) version of the LT1, as base or Formula. Both Trans Ams (base and GT) were fitted with the 275-hp LT1 and six-speed manual transmission. The long tradition of performance options was upheld by the WS6 package: this tag had first

A 1995 Trans Am.

A 2002 Trans Am Firehawk.

appeared back in 1978 as a handling package, and it offered the same option in the mid-1990s, with larger wheels and tires, stiffer suspension, larger stabilizer bars, and four-wheel disc brakes. By 1996, the LT1 V8 had been boosted to 305 hp (227.5 kW) at 5,400 rpm, which, according to *Motor Trend,* allowed the WS6-equipped Trans Am to accelerate to 60 mph (96.5 km/h) in 5.7 seconds and make the quarter-mile in 14 seconds dead. In short, the latest Trans Am was just as quick as the old ones, and complaints that the glory days of performance were over were simply wrong. That was underlined in 1998, when the LT1 was uprated again, this time to 320 hp (238.5 kW) and 345 lb ft (467.8 Nm), enough for a 0–60 mph time of 5.1 seconds.

The following year was the Trans Am's 30th anniversary, and once again Pontiac made the most of its heritage. A limited run of both coupes and convertibles left the production line in white, with two blue racing stripes, just like the 1969 original. There were white leather seats and blue-tinted 17-in (3.2-cm) wheels. Meanwhile, the Firehawk remained the performance flagship. It was still built by SLP Engineering (which had produced the original Firehawk a decade earlier). By 2002, this was offering 345 hp (257 kW) and 350 lb ft (474.6 Nm) from its LS1 V8, 17-in Firestone low-profile tires, spoilers, and 9-in (22.86-cm) aluminum wheels. The Firehawk was not actually a model in its own right, but an option package that could be applied to a Firebird Formula, or the Trans Am coupe or convertible.

In 2002, the Firebird, Trans Am, and Firehawk were all still in production, though there was talk of Pontiac dropping all three later that year. That would have finally closed a 30-year run of the longest-lived muscle car of them all— the great survivor. What was certain was that an all-new Pontiac GTO was on the way, due to be launched in late 2003. Whatever happened to the Firebird, this would be Pontiac's new performance flagship for the 21st century.

This 2002 Trans Am is at the starting line of a drag race.

TEXT- DEPENDENT QUESTIONS

1. How many Trans Ams and Firebirds were sold in 1979?

2. What things were added to the Trans Am for its tenth birthday?

3. When did the fifth-generation Firebirds/Trans Ams appear?

RESEARCH PROJECT

Write a one-page essay explaining why muscle cars are an important part of America's cultural heritage.

This convertible 2002 Trans Am is a striking example of a modern muscle car.

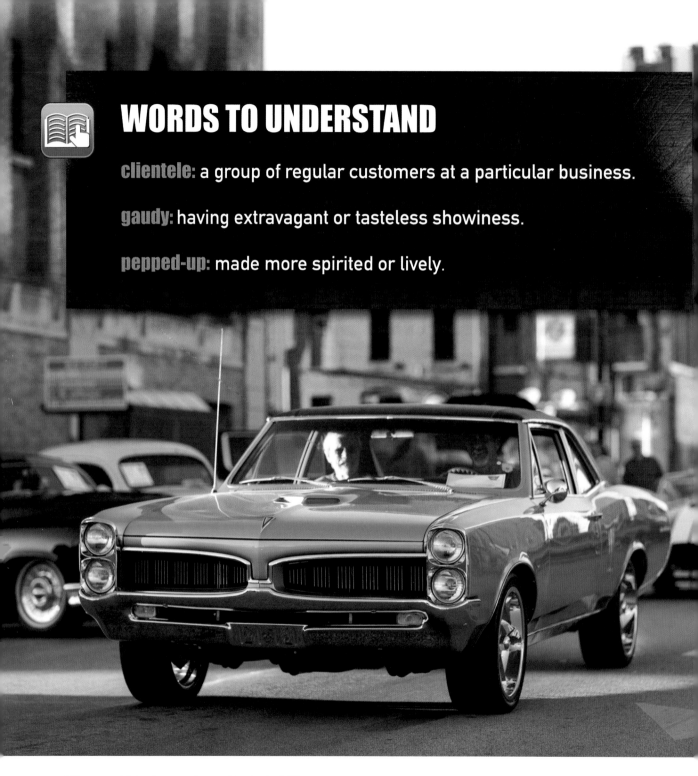

WORDS TO UNDERSTAND

clientele: a group of regular customers at a particular business.

gaudy: having extravagant or tasteless showiness.

pepped-up: made more spirited or lively.

When we think of a muscle car, Pontiac's GTO usually springs to mind. However, there are many other cars that also fall into the category.

CHAPTER 5
OTHER MUSCLE CARS

G TO, Mustang, Hemi, Trans Am, Firebird: these are the muscle cars everyone knows, but there are plenty of others. The "Big Three," plus American Motors, all produced a great deal of muscular metal in the 1960s and 1970s. Some were hardly worthy of the name, and most were mildly **pepped-up** versions of existing cars; but all had performance as a primary aim. This chapter does not attempt to cover all of these, for that would fill an entire book; it aims simply to describe a representative selection.

The Ford Mustang is one of the most famous muscle cars.

BUICK: THE GRAN SPORT

William Mitchell, so the story goes, wanted to create an American Jaguar. As General Motors's head of styling, he liked the way Jaguars combined sportiness with luxury in a sedan package. The new Riviera of 1963 was not that, but the Gran Sport derivative, which appeared a couple of years later, was much closer. In contrast to other Buicks and, for that matter, most other American cars, the Gran Sport came with just one engine and transmission option. But it did not need alternatives as the 425-cu in (6.96-liter) V8, with its 10.25:1 compression, produced 360 hp (268.5 kW), and a massive 465 lb ft (630.5 Nm) of torque. According to *Car and Driver*, its three-speed automatic was "without question, the best automatic transmission in the world."

Twin four-barrel Carter carburetors and big dual exhausts pointed to the power ambitions of this Detroit Jag. There were suspension changes, too: a front anti-roll bar and stiffer springs and shocks all round. All this, and a time of 7.2 seconds for 0–60 mph (0.96.5 km/h), made the Gran Sport a fully fledged muscle car.

In that same year of 1965, Buick unveiled the Skylark GS (Gran Sport). This was a direct response to Pontiac's GTO, being smaller than the Riviera. In fact, "direct response" is quite an appropriate phrase: an early GS advertisement

A 1967 Buick Riviera.

described the car as "your own personal-type nuclear deterrent!" It was not quite as forceful as the big-engined Riviera, but the 401-cu in (6.57-liter) Wildcat power unit allowed 325 hp (242 kW) and 0–60 mph (0-96.5 km/h) in 7.8 seconds. It was also held back by a two-speed automatic and just one four-barrel carburetor.

GS buyers had a choice of six different rear axle ratios, however, and the car could be coaxed into impressive drag strip performance. *Motor Trend* tested one with a 4.3:1 rear end, racing slicks, headers, shimmed front springs, and a transmission kick-down switch. It responded with a standing quarter-mile of 14 seconds at 101 mph (162.5 km/h), reaching 60 mph in 5.7 seconds.

Well aware of the growing interest in muscle cars, Buick upped the GS's power with a 340-hp (253.5-kW)

The GS 455 engine of the Riviera Gran Sport.

option introduced later in the year: even without special tires and ratios, that could trip the lights at just under 15 seconds. In fact, the muscle trend was spreading right across the division, and in 1966 Buick offered a GS version of the full-sized Wildcat, complete with heavy-duty suspension, Positraction, and the 340-hp V8.

Meanwhile, the Skylark GS range was expanded with the cheaper 340, with a 340-cu in (5.57-liter) motor giving 260 hp (194 kW) at 4,200 rpm and a useful 365 lb ft (494.9 Nm) at 2,800 rpm. The engine was a common fitment to mid-sized Buicks at the time, but in the GS 340 came with a four-speed manual gearbox, red stripes, badges, and hood scoops to leave no one in any doubt that this was a budget muscle car. Most buyers (4 to 1) went for the GS 400, and the 340 was soon replaced by the slightly beefier GS 350.

For buyers of muscle cars, the 400 was still the Buick to have, especially in 1967, when it received a brand-new 400-cu in (6.555-liter) engine. Of lighter weight and with better breathing than the old Wildcat motor, it was slightly oversquare, though the claimed power was no different from that of the 340-hp Wildcat. To match it, GS 400 buyers (the car was now a model in its own right) could opt for the latest variable-pitch-stator Super Turbine transmission for an extra $237, which until then had only been available on the big Buicks. But the four-speed manual option was still the fastest: it was a full second quicker to 60 mph (96.5 km/h), for example.

Reflecting these muscular times, the 400 was getting **gaudy**, with more stripes, side vents, and hood scoops, and one could pay $90 extra for chrome-plated wheels. Its performance was getting more serious, too. For 1969, there were two optional levels of tune. Stage I was dealer-fitted, a comprehensive list of parts that included a high-lift cam,

For 1971, the GS became the flashier GSX. It was very different from Buick's earlier models.

high-output oil pump, heavy-duty valve springs, and tubular (thus lighter) pushrods. A large dual exhaust and modified Quadrajet carburetor were part of the package, as were a 5,200 rpm governor in the transmission to prevent over-revving, and a choice of 3.64 or 3.42:1 Positraction rear axles. Pay a little more, and one could have heavy-duty suspension and power front disc brakes as well. Fitted up and ready to go, the GS Stage I produced 345 hp (257 kW) at 4,800 rpm. Stage II was intended only for racing and was not recommended for use on the street or for any car with a silencer. The Buick dealer was not even able to fit the parts: they had to be bought over the counter, from which point the buyer was on his own. That year, a GS 400 was the fastest car tested by *Car Life* magazine and achieved 0–60 mph in 6.1 seconds.

But cubic inches were the final front in the muscle car wars, and Buick obliged in 1970 with the Gran Sport 455. This latest 455-cu in (7.46-liter) V8 was a stretched version of the 430 and produced 350 hp (261 kW) at 4,600 rpm, breaking the 500-lb ft (678-Nm) barrier too at 510 lb ft (691.6 Nm) at 2,800 rpm. That was in a relatively mild state of tune (single four-barrel carburetor and 10.0:1 compression), but once again Stage I was ready and waiting. For a little under $200, buyers could have extra-large valves, big-port cylinder heads, stronger valve springs, a high-lift cam, a modified carburetor, and even blue-printed pistons. Rallye Ride stiffer suspension cost just $15.80 extra: Buick seemed determined to give the horsepower fanatics a good deal! They would not have been disappointed either, as the Stage I GS could rocket to 60 mph (96.5 km/h) in 5.5 seconds and over the quarter-mile in less than 14 seconds. Not surprisingly, these Stage I 455s were popular, making up more than one in fou Buick sales in 1970.

But all of these GS Buicks, however impressive their performance, still looked quite subtle, even understated, compared with the more garish muscle cars, but Buick responded with the GSX; bright yellow with rear spoiler, a black hood, and rally stripes, this was really a GS (with either the 350-hp/261-kW V8 or Stage I) in a flashy new suit, plus all the performance options: a hood-mounted tachometer, power front disc brakes, a four-speed manual box, bucket seats, a stiffer suspension—the list went on. Fewer than 700 GSXs were sold in 1970, suggesting that Buick's traditional **clientele** preferred the classy look, but that did not prevent the company from offering the GSX package on any Gran Sport in 1971–72 as well.

The Gran Sports were tamed and detuned in the early 1970s, but 1982 saw a new generation of Buick muscle cars. The Regal Grand National (to commemorate Buick's NASCAR win) was actually built for Buick by Cars & Concepts of Michigan. As standard, it came with a flabby 4.1-liter V6 of 125 hp (93 kW), but a few cars were fitted with the Regal Sport Coupe's turbocharged 232-cu in (3.8-liter) V6, boasting 175 hp (130.5 kW). The idea behind the turbo was to provide something closer to V8 power with V6 economy. The figures may have looked pale next to a late-1960s muscle car, though of course they were SAE net rather than gross; but by 1987 the V6 was intercooled and delivering 245 hp (183 kW) and 355 lb ft (481.4 Nm), powering a range of all-black Buicks.

The GSX was not as popular as earlier models.

A late-1960s Oldsmobile 442.

OLDSMOBILE: THE 442

If there was one thing that helped to keep General Motors healthy in the 1960s, it was the competition encouraged among its divisions. They shared some components, of course, and that made economic sense for all concerned, but as far as sales went, they were left to sink or swim on their own. Apart from the odd directive from top brass (such as the banning of triple carburetors on any GM car except the Corvette), they were left strictly alone.

So, as soon as Pontiac launched the GTO package, its sibling rivals lost little time in coming up with GTOs of their own. Buick had the Skylark Gran Sport, so what would Oldsmobile have? The answer was the 442. Those numbers would be as evocative to muscle car fans as GTO or even 409. Officially, they stood for four-barrel carburation, four-on-the-floor, and two dual exhausts. At least, they did until the four-speed manual gearbox could be replaced by an optional automatic, and then Oldsmobile claimed that the second "4" represented cubic inches.

Like GTO, the 442 started out as an option package, in this case "Option B-09 Police Apprehender Pursuit," to give it its full official title. A $285 option on the Oldsmobile Cutlass, this brought 310 hp (231 kW), an increase of 20 hp (14.9 kW), as a result of a high-lift cam and high compression, that four-speed manual and dual exhaust. There were also heavy-duty shocks and springs and a rear stabilizer bar. As well as being as fast as a GTO, the 442 rapidly gained the reputation of being the best-handling muscle car of all, an accolade it retained right through the 1960s.

Word soon got around, and the 442 became a popular option, especially from 1965, when Oldsmobile shoehorned in a bigger 400-cu in (6.555-liter) engine: this was a downsized version of Oldsmobile's new 425-cu in (6.96-liter) motor, and incidentally had the added benefit of more cubic inches than the 389-cu in (6.375-liter) unit in the GTO. In practice, it meant 345 hp (257 kW) at 4,800 rpm and a hefty 440 lb ft (596.6 Nm) of torque, enough for a 0–60-mph (0-96.5-km/h) time of 5.5 seconds and a standing quarter-mile of exactly 15 seconds. *Car and Driver* loved it ("a very worthwhile balance of all the qualities we'd like to see incorporated in every American car"), and so did the buying public: just over 25,000 of them ordered the 442 package that year.

For 1966, the Cutlass was restyled, while the 442 package now included convenience features like two-speed wipers and bucket seats. Another 5 hp (3.7 kW) was coaxed out of the V8, thanks to a higher compression, but the big performance news was an optional triple two-barrel carburetor set-up, which claimed 360 hp (268.5 kW). This was Tri-Power, but it was only available for a year before the GM management handed down the banning order. Still, the standard 350-hp (261-kW) 442 in 1967 was surely fast enough, especially when it cost a mere $184 extra. As well as the engine, it brought heavy-duty suspension, wheels, and engine mounts, wide, low-profile tires, and those desirable little red "442" badges. If one insisted, the bucket seats could be swapped for a good old-fashioned bench

A 1970s Oldsmobile 442 convertible.

LEFT: This 442 has a vinyl roof, known as a holiday hardtop.

BELOW: A 442 convertible.

seat. That year, the 442 option was available on all Cutlass Supreme two-door cars, which indicated its popularity.

But the 442 had become such a strong badge that, just like the GTO, it was made a model in its own right. For 1968, the 442 was still a hopped-up Cutlass but was not badged as such. There were three of them: holiday hardtop, sports coupe, and convertible, all with a new 400-cu in (6.555-liter) engine in 325-, 350-, and 360-hp (242-, 261-, and 268.5-kW) forms. The last gave the same power as the triple-carburetor Tri-Power, but Oldsmobile got around the ban by finding the extra power in a different way. It was almost as if there were unspoken warfare between the top bureaucrats and the designers on the shop floor.

There was another way to avoid GM bans: team up with an outside supplier. That is what Oldsmobile did with famed tuner George Hurst. Hurst had already squeezed Oldsmobile's biggest 455-cu in (7.46-liter) motor into a 442,

and this so impressed Oldsmobile that dealer John Demmer of Michigan was persuaded to build replicas, and being dealer specials, no GM power limitations could apply! This car was the first in a long line of Hurst/Oldsmobiles, which used the standard 442 base with a Force Air 455 supplying 390 hp (291 kW) and 500 lb ft (678 Nm). The engine itself was special, based on that of the Tornado but with special crank, high-lift/duration cam, Ram Air cylinder heads, and a modified auto transmission: this last was equipped with a Hurst Dual-Gate shifter that could be operated either manually or left to itself. It was quick, according to *Super Stock* magazine, to the tune of a 12.9-second quarter-mile, tripping the lights at 109 mph (175 km/h).

The hottest factory 442 remained the W30, which had started out as a drag-racing special but was now firmly aimed at the man in the street, though with optional rear axles down to 4.66:1, it is fair to say that many W30s ended up on the strip anyway. Little cosmetic touches underlined the 360-hp (268.5-kW) W30's status: bucket seats, red stripe tires, and hood stripes. There was also a slightly milder W31 package for 1969, with a Turbo Hydra-Matic transmission, but this made up only one percent of Oldsmobile's sales that year. For 1970, the W30 package also included 10.88-in (27.64-cm) front discs as well as the familiar Ram Air induction system, for which Oldsmobile claimed only an extra 5 hp (3.7 kW) over the standard 442. What everyone agreed on was that the 442 was still the muscle car of choice for handling.

But times were changing, and 1971 was the last year for the 442 as a separate model: just like the GTO, changing times brought a decline in popularity, and the first sign that the manufacturers were aware of this was a reversion of these muscle car models to option packages rather than being models in their own right.

By the end of the 1970s, the wild times of 360-hp (268.5-kW) 455-cu in (7.46-liter) 442s must have seemed a distant memory indeed, but in 1979, there was an attempt to inject a little of the old excitement back into the new downsized Cutlass. For around $2,000 (a lot of money on top of a $5,631 base price), buyers received a bigger 350-cu in (5.735-liter) V8 of 170 hp (127 kW) in place of the standard 130-hp (100-5-kW) 305 unit, with a gold paint job, gold aluminum wheels, and a Hurst Dual-Gate shifter on the auto transmission. In sanitized form, the Hurst/Oldsmobile lived on. In fact, so strong was the name that it returned for 1984, complete with a three-lever Lightning Rod Automatic Shifter, 180-hp (134-kW) 307-cu in (5.03-liter) V8, heavy-duty suspension, and fat tires: it sold 3,500 in that year and was the most popular Hurst/Oldsmobile ever.

CHEVROLET: THE CHEVELLE

Just as Oldsmobile quickly responded to the GTO threat in 1964, so did Chevrolet, though at first it was turned down by General Motors's top management. The concept of a biggish V8 bolted into a mid-sized car had obviously worked so well for Pontiac that GM's "cheap car" division wanted to do the same. Oldsmobile had lost no time in turning the Cutlass, with a police-specification engine and suspension, into the famed 442. Chevrolet, not unreasonably, decided to fit its small-block 327-cu in (5.36-liter) engine into the Chevelle. Inexplicably, the concept was turned down: the 327 was actually mild by comparison with the 310-hp (231-kW) Oldsmobile unit, let alone the GTO's 325-hp (242-kW) 389-cu in (6.375-liter) motor.

Fortunately for Chevrolet, head office relented, and the Chevelle SS 327 was born. The Chevelle actually made a good base for a muscle car. First of all, it was cheap, the lowest priced of GM's four A-body mid-sized cars. There was already a Super Sport (SS) option with bucket seats, console, and badging, but with a maximum of 220 hp (164 kW) from the biggest V8 available, it was no GTO scarer. Finally, the small-block 327 would slot straight in, and the engine itself was a proven quantity. So, in the middle of that 1964 model year, two new options joined the Chevelle's list: the L30 (250-hp/186.5-kW) and L74 (300-hp/224-kW) versions of the 327, costing $95 and $138, respectively, over the base 283-cu in (4.64-liter) V8. In theory, one could even have the Corvette's hot 365-hp (272-kW) version of this engine, the L76, but it is thought that these super-Chevelles went in limited quantities only to drag racers.

So, the Chevelle had its muscle derivative at last, but it was not really strong enough to challenge a GTO or 442. For that, it needed a big-block motor, and that was not long in coming. Not that it was just a case of slotting Chevrolet's 396-cu in (6.49-liter) engine straight into the Chevelle. In fact, it was so awkward that in its first year that Chevrolet did not even advertise the fact that a 396 Chevelle was available, preferring to sell it in very limited numbers.

The problem was that to fit the big-block was expensive and time-consuming. A convertible frame was used with a coupe body, with two extra body mounts, and rear suspension reinforcements. Special left- and right-hand exhaust

A 1967 Chevelle Malibu convertible.

A 1969 Chevelle SS.

manifolds had to be made to squeeze the bigger engine in. Bigger power-assisted brakes (11-in/27.9-cm drums all round) were fitted, as were stiffer springs and shocks, plus stronger hubs and wider wheels. Even the Chevelle's ring-gear had to be swapped for a bigger one, and the engineers also added a bigger 11-in (27.9-cm) clutch and four-speed Muncie gearbox. Just 201 of these Chevelle "Z16" SS396s were built for 1965, so it was not possible for a prospective purchaser to stroll into his local Chevrolet dealer, order one, and expect immediate delivery. No matter, Chevrolet had made its intention clear.

This intention was made clearer still in the following year, when the rebodied Chevelle came as an SS396 from the start. In fact, there were three of them. The base 396 (it was a de-stroked version of the famous 409) produced 325 hp (242 kW) at 4,800 rpm and 410 lb ft (556 Nm). If that was not enough, one could opt for the 360-hp (268.5-kW) L34. This had lots of internal changes: a higher-lift cam, chrome piston rings, a forged alloy crankshaft, and dual exhaust, though it was only slightly torquier than the base L35, majoring on that substantial power increase. Still not enough? Then there was the top L78 with hotter-still cam, 11.0:1 compression, and other parts to give 375 hp (279.5 kW) at 5,600 rpm. That could reach 60 mph (96.5 km/h) in an alleged 6.5 seconds, but the L78 was in a very high state of tune, and it is thought that only around 100 Chevelles were equipped with it. The point was that a big-block Chevelle out-cubed the GTO and was now available at any Chevrolet dealer, in four-speed manual or automatic form, sport coupe, or convertible. Together, over 72,000 of these were built in 1966, with another 63,000 in the following year.

The engine range was trimmed in 1967, though. The base engine was still the 325-hp L35, while the L34 was derated to 350 hp (26 1kW) at 5,200 rpm. As for the top-powered L78, this 375-hp unit was not available as a factory option anymore, but one could buy all the necessary parts at a local dealer. Whatever the engine choice, a Chevelle 396 came with a three- or four-speed manual gearbox, or a Powerglide automatic, with no fewer than nine rear axle ratios available, between 3.07:1 and 4.10:1. With the 350-hp motor and the 4.88:1 axle, one could turn in some impressive performances on the drag strip.

For 1969, the 375-hp option was back, a clear sign of the times that the muscle car war was hotting up: 350 hp as top power just was not sufficient anymore. The Chevelle had a new body that year, the popular long hood/short deck look, with a fastback on the coupe, though sales slid again to 57,000. For 1970, the SS396 reverted to option-package status rather than being a model in its own right. Normally, this is a signifier of low and falling sales, but that year they rocketed right back up to over 86,000, the best yet for the Chevelle SS.

Smart but not flashy, the package brought lots of detail items to differentiate the SS from lesser Chevelles: twin hood bulges, a black grille, bright wheel rims, roof drip moldings, rally stripes, and white-letter F70 x 14 tires with 7-in (17.8-cm) sports wheels. At $440, it was still good value, especially as the heart of the 396 was now the 350-hp engine, with a new 375-hp unit with aluminum heads (and probably more power than was claimed) as the top option.

A 1970 Chevelle SS.

A 1971 Chevelle.

Or was it? Through GM's infamous Central Office Production Order (COPO) system, it was possible to order a Chevelle with even more power, direct from the factory. COPO (as detailed in the Camaro chapter) was intended as a means of satisfying fleet managers who wanted non-standard specification cars; for example, a bench seat in place of standard buckets, or a cheaper three-speed gearbox instead of a four-speeder. But if one knew the system, it could be used to order big-block engines. Chevrolet dealer Don Yenko did just that with the 427-cu in (7.0-liter) big-block V8, and some of these found their way into very special Chevelle SS427s. Yenko even converted 30 lightweight Novas with COPO-procured 427s and later admitted that the result was "a beast, almost lethal," capable of reaching 60 mph in less than 4 seconds. The insurance companies agreed: they refused to cover the Nova 427, and no more were converted.

Chevrolet's Monte Carlo could not have been more different. Launched in 1970 as a luxury two-door, it was really an extended Chevelle. From the muscle point of view, the Monte Carlo's most significant feature was its SS454 package, which used Chevrolet's new 454-cu in (7.44-liter) version of the Turbo Jet big-block V8. This came in a mild state of tune—a 10.25:1 compression ratio and a single Rochester four-barrel carburetor—but still pushed out 360 hp (268.5 kW) at a relaxed 4,400 rpm, plus 500 lb ft (678 Nm) at 3,200 rpm. Still, the Monte Carlo was not really marketed as a muscle car, and this explain in part at least why only 2.6 percent of them were ordered with the SS package and big motor.

In that same year, Chevrolet did the obvious thing and slotted the 454 into the Chevelle. It was obvious because the car had built up quite a reputation as one of the leading muscle cars, and even the top 396s were starting to get left behind by the 400-hp (298-kW) opposition. Chevelle SS454 buyers had a choice of two tunes: they could have the motor in its soft Monte Carlo form, nice and lazy, with bags of torque at low revs. But of more interest to the muscle car crowd was the LS6 version, with a higher 11.25:1 compression, bigger 780-cfm (22.09-m³/minute) Holley four-barrel carburetor, big exhaust valves, and solid lifters. All told, it came to 450 hp (335.5 kW) at 5,600 rpm and had the same peak torque as the softer LS5. To cope with the extra power, there were four-bolt main bearings, nodular iron bearing caps, and heavy-duty con rods. Together, they could shift the Chevelle to 60 mph (96.5 km/h) in just 5.4 seconds and turn in a quarter-mile in the high 13 seconds. It is little wonder that collectors see this as the ultimate Chevelle muscle car.

But this was the turning point. Insurance problems with high-powered muscle cars, in combination with new emissions and safety legislation, meant that the days of cars like the SS454 were numbered. For 1971, Chevrolet took the significant step of making the SS package (the stripes, suspension, and show-off bits) available on lower-powered 350 and 400 V8s as well as on the 454. It was the right move, as over three-quarters of SS buyers chose the smaller engines that year. By 1972, one could even get a Chevelle SS307, while the 450-hp 454 had gone. The remaining 454 was detuned, with lower compression and 270 hp (201 kW) net, but Chevrolet sold only 2,500 of this model in 1973. This was no longer what people wanted.

1972 Chevelle SS. By 1972, the double headlights were replaced with singles.

A 1965 Plymouth Barracuda at a classic car event.

PLYMOUTH/DODGE: BARRACUDA/DART

Plymouth's Barracuda of the late 1960s and early 1970s, the hell-raising Hemi-powered 'Cuda that was tricky to insure, was a quintessential muscle car. But the original Barracuda was not like that at all. It started out in 1964 as a mild-mannered fastback version of the Valiant sedan. "We are sure," said Plymouth's general manager P.N. Buckminster, "that the Plymouth Barracuda is just right for young, sports-minded Americans who want to enjoy the fun of driving a car that also fulfills their general transportation needs." And that summed it up. The first Barracuda was a wholesome, sensible, fun car, though its degree of wholesomeness depended on what one got up to on the fold-down rear seat: "7 feet of fully carpeted "anything" space."

Although it was Plymouth's response to the Mustang, the Barracuda was in no way a hot car. There was just one V8 option, a 273-cu in (4.47-liter) unit with a single two-barrel carburetor and mild 180 hp (134 kW), though a four-speed manual gearbox with Hurst shifter was optional. This was not what mid-1960s America wanted, and sure enough, only 23,000 Barracudas were sold in their first eight months.

But Plymouth realized what was holding back sales and rushed a revamped 'Cuda into production. Now the 273 V8 came with a four-barrel carburetor, a 10.5:1 compression ratio, and 235 hp (175 kW). The four-speed box was still an option but could now make the car sprint to 60 mph (96.5 km/h) in 8.2 or 9.1 seconds, depending on which magazine was doing the driving. To go with the hotter V8, a Formula S package brought wide wheels and tires, stiffer suspension, and rally stripes. This was more in tune with the market, and over 64,000 were sold.

A Dodge Dart 340.

That success encouraged Plymouth to make the Barracuda a model in its own right for 1967, and introduce a still-more-powerful engine, this one a 383-cu in (6.28-liter) V8 pushing out 280 hp (209 kW) with its Carter four-barrel carburetor and a 10.0:1 compression. Front disc brakes, bucket seats, and a Sure-Grip differential were among the options, plus, of course, the inevitable rally stripes. Once again, over 60,000 Barracudas were sold, making these warmed up versions more popular than the hot and hairy 'Cudas ever were.

The Barracuda grew out of the Valiant, Plymouth's compact car. Fellow Chrysler division, Dodge, had its own compact, the Dart, and this became a formidable mini-muscle car for a few years in the late 1960s. Announced in 1968, the Dart GTS (it stood for "GT Sport") was Dodge's equivalent of the Plymouth Road Runner, though unlike that mini-muscle, it never received the legendary Hemi power unit. But, as it turned out, what it had was quite enough.

GTS buyers had the choice of two V8s. The 340-cu in (5.57-liter) small-block had a bore and stroke of 4.04 x 3.31 in (102.6 x 84.1 mm); with 10.5:1 compression and a single four-barrel carburetor, it could push out a respectable 275 hp (205 kW) at 5,000 rpm and 340 lb ft (461Nm) at 3,200 rpm. Alternatively, one could have a 383-cu in (6.28-liter) big-block with 300 hp (224 kW), which was a lot of power for a compact. To go with the big V8, the GTS brought what Dodge described as Rallye suspension, 14 x 5.5-in wheels, and Red Streak tires; most cars were also ordered with a four-speed manual gearbox with a Hurst shifter, or a competition-type TorqueFlite automatic. And being part of the Dodge "Scat Pack" (applied to the Charger R/T and Coronet R/T as well as the GTS), there were rear-end bumblebee stripes and hood power bulges.

There was little need for the little Dart to persuade anyone it were quick: 6 seconds was claimed for the 0–60-mph (0–96.5-km/h) sprint, and 15.2 seconds for the quarter-mile. If anything, those claims were slightly modest, as *Hot Rod* magazine recorded a 14.38-second quarter-mile in a TorqueFlite GTS. It got even faster in 1969, when the 383 V8 was uprated to 330 hp (246 kW), though the GTS remained a minority interest, with fewer than 7,000 (both hardtops and convertibles) sold in that year.

More popular was the Dart Swinger 340. This was an unashamed budget muscle car that gave performance great priority and luxury very little. "Dart Swinger 340," went the advertisement, "Newest member of the Dodge Scat Pack. You get 340 cubes of high-winding, 4-barrel V8. A 4-speed Hurst shifter on the floor to keep things moving. All other credentials are in order." And they were: the Swinger had just as much power and performance as the GTS, not to mention the Rallye suspension, wide wheels, and bumblebee stripes. One could not have a convertible, and full carpeting only came if the four-speed was specified.

But who cared? At less than $3,000, the Swinger gave more performance per dollar than almost anything else, and Dodge sold 20,000 of them in 1969. Nor was a low price the only attraction: the Swinger proved cheaper to insure than other muscle cars with the same performance, as the insurance companies considered it a true compact car

A 1969 Plymouth Barracuda doing a burnout at the starting line before a drag racing competition.

A 1973 Barracuda 340.

and thus a better risk. Presumably they had not seen the performance figures: 6.5 seconds to 60 mph (96.5 km/h) and the standing quarter-mile in around 14.5 seconds could be expected. Scat Pack, indeed.

By 1971, the Dart had moved on. The year before, Plymouth had enjoyed great success with the Valiant Duster compact, and now it was Dodge's turn. So, the 108-in (2.74-m) wheelbase coupe variant became a new Dodge for 1971, the Demon. Economy-minded motorists could order one of these with a 198-cu in (3.24-liter) six, but of more interest to muscle car fans was the small-block 340 V8, which took on that 275-hp motor that had done such good service in the Dart GTS and Swinger. The add-ons were much the same: standard three-speed manual transmission, with a four-speeder or TorqueFlite auto optional. Heavy-duty suspension, Rallye instrument cluster, E70-14 tires, stripes, and dual exhaust were all part of the package as well. If they did not make a big enough statement, then the optional black hood with two gaping air scoops, a rear spoiler or "Tuff" steering wheel, surely would.

Motor Trend tested a Demon 340 against a Mercury Comet GT, Chevrolet Nova SS 350 and AMC Hornet SC360. The Demon was the heaviest of the lot, at 3,360 lb (1524 kg), but also the quickest, with a standing quarter-mile time of 14.49 seconds and a time of 6.5 seconds to 60 mph (96.5 km/h). For 1972, the 340's compression was lowered to 8.5:1, though the power drop to 240 hp (179 kW) was not as drastic as it seemed: it was now measured on the SAE net rating. Whatever, it still made an affordable muscle car and was certainly easier to insure than its bigger brothers. Interestingly, the car carried on into 1976, but the "Demon" name did not. Religious groups took exception to it, and from 1973 the Demon was renamed the Dart Sport.

The Comet Cyclone was considered Mercury's answer to a muscle car.

FORD: COUGAR & 427S

One would have expected Mercury, maker of luxury, upscale Fords, to have been above the whole muscle car thing, but not a bit of it: there were performance Mercuries right through the 1960s. They may not have been as flashy as some (all those stripes, wings, and spoilers were not really in Mercury's marketplace), but they were there. Take the Comet Cyclone, a powered-up version of the standard Comet. For 1966, the Cyclone GT (based on Ford's Fairlane) was selected as the Indy 500 pace car (a sure sign of performance pretensions). Powered by Ford's 335-hp (250-kW) 390-cu in (6.4-liter) V8, complete with handling package and front disc brakes, it could do the quarter-mile in the high 14 seconds. So, it was fast enough, though only around 16,000 were sold.

The Cougar, launched in 1967, promised to have more mass appeal. *Car Life* magazine described it as a "Mustang with class," and that is exactly what it was. The Cougar was based firmly on the pony car floorpan, but with its own body shell and tweaked suspension to provide a more comfortable ride. As far as buyers of muscle cars were concerned, the most serious Cougar was the GT 390. This made use of the same 390-cu in V8 as the Cyclone GT, and in the same relatively mild state of tune with three- or four-speed manual gearboxes or a three-speed Merc-O-Matic. Having softened up the suspension for standard Cougars, Mercury firmed it back up for the GT: stiffer springs, beefier shocks, and a larger front anti-roll bar, plus power front disc brakes and wider tires. But the Cougar was not particularly fast (8.1 seconds to 60 mph/96.5 km/h and 16 seconds for the quarter-mile), and the fact that almost half were sold with the three-speed manual or auto suggested that many were being bought by non-sporting customers.

A late 1960s Cougar.

Things got more serious in 1968, with the 427-cu in (7.0-liter) GT-E, giving 390 hp (291 kW) in a fairly mild state of tune, rapidly superseded by the 428 Cobra Jet. Ford actually quoted only 335 hp (250 kW) for the new engine, but this was probably a ploy to make the performance Fords and Mercuries cheaper to insure. It is more likely that power was around the same as that of the 427 it replaced. Mercury was now getting serious about racing, and entered the Trans Am series at around this time. One spin-off was the XR-7G: the G stood for "Dan Gurney", and in fact "signature" special editions like this were popular at the time. The XR-7G was really a cosmetic package and could be had with any of the Cougar power units.

By 1970, Mercury's slogan for the Cougar and its new Eliminator fastback derivative was "America's most completely equipped sports car." In keeping with the Mercury badge, it was marketed as a luxury sports car, which by and large it was. There was more noise insulation than in a Mustang, and a better-equipped interior. Although the

engine range was the same as that of the Mustang (including the high-revving Boss 302, the Cleveland 351, 428 CJ, and even the 375-hp/279.5-kW Boss 429), the interior was pure Mercury, especially on the XR-7: vinyl high-back bucket seats with leather accents, map pockets on the seat backs, burr walnut effect on the instrument panel, loop yarn nylon carpeting, an electric clock, a tachometer, a rocker switch display, a rear seat armrest, map and courtesy lights – the list went on.

For 1971, Cougar grew bigger and fatter (it was already larger than the original Mustang), and had now abandoned its pony car roots. Available as the base and sporty XR-7, choices of Cougar engine started with a two-barrel 351-cu in (5.75-liter) motor, offering 240 hp (179 kW). The same engine with a four-barrel carburetor produced 285 hp (212.5 kW), while the top-range 429-cu in (7.0-liter) motor claimed 370 hp (276 kW). It was a far cry from the Mustang, or indeed any other muscle car: it was heavier, with as much emphasis on trim and appointments as sheer performance.

A 1970 Cougar.

That explained why the Cougar was never a major player in the muscle car market, and as the 1960s wore on the same was true for full-sized cars. They were too heavy and unwieldy to compete with a GTO or LS6 Chevelle, the whole basis of the muscle car concept being to squeeze a big engine into a relatively small car. Big engine in big car did not have the same effect.

Throughout the 1960s, however, the bigger Fords were able to turn in fast straight-line speeds as a result of one engine, the 427-cu in "side oiler." This had first appeared in 1963, primarily for NASCAR and drag racing, but Ford also built nearly 5,000 big Galaxies that year with 427 power. They came either in 425-hp (317-kW) street-tune form but with dual four-barrel Holley carburetors, or milder 410-hp (307-kW) form with a single carburetor. Whether for weekend racing or pure road use, in the base Galaxie or 500 XL, the new 427 gave a good account of itself. Heavy the Galaxies may have been, but from the way they scorched off the line many thought that 425 hp was a conservative estimate. Ford itself claimed a 14.9-second standing quarter-mile for the 500XL hardtop 427 in 1965. By then, the engines had names: Thunderbird High Performance and Thunderbird Super High Performance for the 410- and 425-hp units, respectively.

Until 1966, the 427 could be had only in the full-size Galaxie, but for that year the mid-sized Fairlane was redesigned to make room in the engine bay for this big-block. Only about 60 Fairlane 427s were produced in 1966, but unofficial claims of a 14.5-second quarter-mile heightened the anticipation. As it happened, even in 1967 the 427 remained a limited-production option on the Fairlane, most GTs and GTAs leaving the line with Ford's familiar 390-cu in (6.4-liter) unit. Meanwhile, the new Galaxie "7 Liter" received Ford's new 428-cu in (7.0-liter) motor in 345- and 360-hp (257- and 268.5-kW) forms, though one could still pay extra and order the hot 427 in 410- or 425-hp (306- and 317-kW) forms.

From the power point of view, that was the high spot: for 1968, the 427 was detuned to 390 hp (291 kW), and production ended in the middle of that year. The newer Cobra Jet 428 and Thunder Jet 429 were certainly powerful but could not compare with the original 427. Ford's mid-sized muscle-car flag was taken up by these engines in the Torino, the sporty version of the Fairlane 500. That came in stripped-down budget form for $2,699, and although on paper it produced a relatively paltry 335 hp (250 kW), Ford still claimed a 14.5-second quarter-mile as a result of the fact that the Torino was lighter than the big Galaxie. The fastback Talladega Torino, unveiled in the following year to bring NASCAR honors, used the same CJ-428 engine. For 1970, the new 429 motor replaced the 428, promising 360 or 370 hp (268.5 or 276 kW), depending on tune. But the vast majority of buyers went for the cheaper 302-powered car. It was surely a sign of the times.

A Cougar XR7.

TEXT- DEPENDENT QUESTIONS

1. Name three of the most iconic muscle cars.

2. Name two muscle cars made by Buick.

3. What changes were made to the Cougar in 1971?

A Mercury Cougar XR-7.

A 1973 Mercury Cougar waiting for a new owner.

RESEARCH PROJECT

Compare and contrast today's muscle cars with those of the 1960s, 1970s, and 1980s.

acceleration	The process of moving faster or an increase in velocity.
aerodynamic	How efficiently an object is able to move through the air.
air scoop	An air inlet on the outer surface of automobile use to maintain a flow of air to a power plant or a ventilating system.
bodyshell	The outer casing of an automobile body, excluding doors, window glass, other fittings, and components.
camshaft	A shaft to which a cam is joined.
carburetor	A piece of apparatus for premixing vaporized fuel and air and supplying the mixture to an automobile's engine.
cylinder head	The closed end of a pump cylinder or automobile engine.
concept car	An automobile built to present a new design or technology.
crankshaft	A metal structure that connects an automobile's engine to the wheels enabling them to turn.
coupe	A two-door automobile, usually designed for two persons.
disc brakes	A brake operated by disc surfaces that rub together in the form of discs.
drag race	A competition in which drivers race vehicles at high speeds over a short, specified distance.
emissions	Substances discharged into the air by an automobile engine.
fastback	An automobile with a long, curving, and downward-sloping roof.
flagship	The most important one in a group—often used before another noun.
fuel injection	An electronically controlled system for injecting fuel into an automobile's engine.
gas-guzzler	An automobile that gets relatively poor mileage per gallon.
hardtop	An automobile with a permanent, rigid roof.
horsepower	A unit of power.
hot rod	An automobile rebuilt or modified for high speeds and power.
muscle car	Any of a group of American-made automobiles with powerful engines designed for high-performance driving.
NASCAR	National Association for Stock Car Auto Racing.
performance car	A sports car.
pickup truck	A light truck with an enclosed cab and an open body with low sides and tailgate.
piston	An engine part that slides back and forth inside a larger cylinder.
pony car	A type of two-door hardtop car with sporty styling and high performance.
production line	A line of machines operated by workers in a factory.
rear spoiler	An air deflector placed on the rear of an automobile to reduce lift at high speeds.
sedan	A two- or four-door automobile seating four or more persons and usually with an enclosed roof.
shock absorber	A device for absorbing the energy of sudden impulses or shocks in an automobile.
suspension	A system of springs supporting the upper part of an automobile on the axles.
tachometer	A device that measures how speed or velocity.
turbocharge	To supercharge an automobile's engine by means of a turbine-driven compressor.
torque	A force that produces or tends to produce rotation or torsion.
vehicle warranty	A promise by a manufacturer or dealer that it will repair or replace defects in an automobile for a specified period of time.

FURTHER READING

Cotter, Tom and Ross, Michael Alan. *Motor City Barn Finds: Detroit's Lost Collector Cars*. Minneapolis, MN. Quarto Publishing Group, 2017.

Farr, Donald. *The Complete Book of Classic Ford and Mercury Muscle Cars*. Minneapolis, MN. Quarto Publishing Group, 2018.

Glastonbury, Jim. *Muscle Cars: Style, Power, and Performance*. Minneapolis, MN. Quarto Publishing Group, 2017.

Glatch, Tom. *The Complete Book of American Supercars*. Minneapolis, MN. Quarto Publishing Group, 2016.

McIntosh, Dale. *The Definitive Chevelle SS*. Forest Lake, MN. CarTech Inc., 2018.

INTERNET RESOURCES

https://www.caranddriver.com *Car and Driver* is an American automotive enthusiast magazine. Its website offers interesting articles about the world of automobiles.

https://www.autotrader.com *Auto Trader* is an American website used for selling, valuing, and reviewing cars.

https://www.gm.com *General Motors* is a world-famous American car manufacturer. Its website provides useful information about the cars they produce.

https://www.britannica.com/topic/Ford-Motor-Company A useful resource into the history of the *Ford Motor Company*.

https://www.gentlemansgazette.com/muscle-cars-explained-history A useful website explaining the history of the muscle car and also some of the great models.

AUTHOR'S BIOGRAPHY

Nicholas Tomkins is a full-time journalist and photographer specializing in writing articles about classic cars and motorcycles. His work was first published over ten years ago when he worked at a publishing house in London. Following his early career, he went to live in New York for another leading publishing company, where he contributed to hundreds of books, magazines, and television programs. Additionally, Tomkins is an expert in the restoration of muscle cars of the 1960s and 1970s. To his credit, he has painstakingly restored at least four iconic cars to their former glory. Not just satisfied with his own hobby, Tomkins hosts workshops and training days for other would-be classic car restorers. Today, Tomkins lives near Exeter, England, where he works from home. He is married with two children.

PICTURE & VIDEO CREDITS